DISCOVERING DINOSAURS
FLYING MONSTERS

INTERNET LINKED

MICHAEL BENTON

zigzag

⚠️

INTERNET SAFETY
Always follow these guidelines for a fun and safe
journey through cyberspace:

1. Ask your parents for permission before you go online.

2. Spend time with your parents online
and show them your favourite sites.

3. Post your family's e-mail address, even if you have your own
(only give your personal address to someone you trust).

4. Do not reply to e-mails if you feel
they are strange or upsetting.

5. Do not use your real surname while you are online.

6. Never arrange to meet 'cyber friends' in person
without your parents' permission.

7. Never give out your password.

8. Never give out your home address or telephone number.

9. Do not send scanned pictures of yourself
unless your parents approve.

10. Leave a website straight away if you find something that is
offensive or upsetting. Talk to your parents about it.

Every effort has been made to ensure none of the recommended websites in this book is linked to inappropriate material. However, due to the ever-changing nature of the Internet, the publishers regret they cannot take responsibility for future content of these websites. Therefore, it is strongly advised that children and parents consider the safety guidelines above.

First published in the UK in 2002 by Zigzag
an imprint of Chrysalis Children's Books
64 Brewery Road, London N7 9NT

© 2002 Zigzag Children's Books

Author: Prof. Michael Benton
Consultant: Dougal Dixon BSc (Hons), MSc
Illustrator: John Sibbick
Digital Retouch Artist: Steve Sweet

Editorial Director: Honor Head
Art Director: Simon Rosenheim
Senior Editor: Rasha Elsaeed
Project Editor: Jane Yorke
Assistant Editor: Clare Chambers
Project Designer: Sarah Crouch
Assistant Designers: Keren-Orr Greenfeld, Zeta Jones

ISBN 1 903954 27 4

British Library Cataloguing in Publication Data for this book is available from the British Library

Printed and bound in Taiwan

CONTENTS

FIRST BIRDS?

During the age of the dinosaurs, the skies were ruled by the pterosaurs or 'winged reptiles'. Some were the size of pigeons, but others were monster gliders.

Were pterosaurs ancestors of lizards, birds or bats? Fossil evidence shows that pterosaurs appeared at the beginning of the dinosaur age. Scientists think that they are close relatives of the land-living dinosaurs because they had a backbone and upright legs. Pterosaurs may have evolved from the flying reptiles of earlier times. These creatures looked like winged lizards. Birds have also been thought of as modern-day pterosaurs. However, birds appeared halfway through the dinosaur age and are phyiscally similar to the dinosaurs. Like the pterosaurs, birds probably evolved directly from the dinosaurs. Bats appeared after the pterosaurs died out. Yet they have more in common with the prehistoric pterosaurs than birds.

Early fliers
The first pterosaurs appeared during the Triassic Period. They had long wings, prominent wrist bones, pointed teeth, sharp beaks and unusual-shaped heads and jaws.

DINO DICTIONARY

🔘 **Ancestor:** the animal or plant species from which a group arose

🔘 **Evolve:** develop over a long time

Monsters in the sky

The largest pterosaurs appeared in the Cretaceous Period. Many different fliers swirled the skies during this time. Pterosaurs had diversified into different species (types), with different shaped beaks, jaws and head crests to suit their lifestyles.

Jurassic treasures

Most of the information about pterosaurs comes from the huge number of fossils found in the Solnhofen quarries in southern Germany. In the late Jurassic times, Solnhofen was covered by a lagoon filled with stagnant water. It was flanked by mountains to the north and the deeper waters of what is now the Mediterranean Sea. When flying specimens and sea creatures died, they were buried along with the fine sediment that settled at the bottom of the lagoon. The number of perfect fossils found at Solnhofen has made it one of the most treasured sites among fossil scientists.

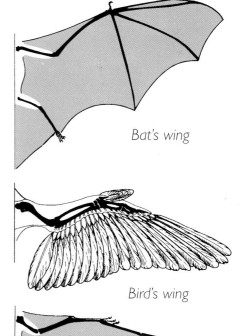

Bat's wing

Bird's wing

Pterosaur's wing

Bird or bat?

A wing has to be a special shape so that an animal can fly. The wings of bats, birds and pterosaurs are similar in shape, but their bone construction is different. This suggests that these animals evolved from different ancestors.

THE WINGED ONES

UP CLOSE

There were two groups of pterosaurs. The rhamphorhynchoids appeared early in the Triassic Period. The second, more advanced group, the pterodactyloids, followed towards the end of the Jurassic Period.

Pterosaurs probably flew like modern birds. Small ones could flap their wings to lift themselves. Larger pterosaurs may have soared on warm air currents. They relied on the shape of their wings to move through the air like gliders. Unlike birds, pterosaur wings were made of skin that stretched along the arm bone. Fossils of pterosaur wing membranes show that the wings were stiffened by rods of gristle that fanned out from the arms. This pattern of rods is similar to the bony structure that supports the feathers on a bird's wing. Paleontologists disagree on how the wings were attached to the pterosaur's body. The wings may have been attached to the trunk, the legs or they may have reached down to the knees or even the ankles.

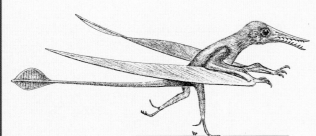

Teeth
The narrow, pointed jaws were lined with different-sized, forward-pointing teeth.

Rhamphorhynchoid features
This group was named after Rhamphorhynchus. It had a slender skeleton, short neck and wrist bones and a long tail. The long, narrow wings consisted of bones of equal lengths.

On the ground
Did pterosaurs run on their back legs like small bird-footed dinosaurs? Scientists once thought that pterosaurs tucked up their wings under their arms to walk on two legs. Fossil footprints later showed that they actually walked on all fours, using their hands on the their wings as well as their feet.

Long tail
The stiff tail, lined with thin bony rods, may have acted as a rudder – for steering or balancing during flight.

Pterodactylus

This is one of the most well-known pterosaurs. Pterodactylus' wings were made up of separate membranes. The main wing membrane was attached to the legs about halfway down. A small membrane was joined to the front of the arm. There may have been a membrane between the legs, below the tail. The wing membranes were stiffened by rods of gristle. These fanned out from the arm and hand.

Pterodactyloid features

The more advanced pterosaurs were named after Pterodactylus. Its skeleton was different to that of Rhamphorhynchus (left). It had a long head and neck, a short tail and the wing bones were of different lengths. The teeth were also much smaller.

Teeth

These varied in size and were adapted for eating particular food. Small fliers with tiny teeth probably ate insects. Bigger ones with larger teeth may have fed on fish or lizards.

Long wrist bone

The wing bones were of different lengths.

RISE OF THE PTEROSAURS

Fossils of the earliest pterosaurs show that from the beginning, they had all the key features that made them successful fliers.

The earliest pterosaur fossils have been found in rocks in Europe that date from the late Triassic Period. They include *Eudimorphodon* and *Peteinosaurus.* Fossils of these early pterosaurs indicate that they had already evolved the main features of a typical pterosaur. They had large wings made from stretchy skin and supported by rods of gristle. Each wing was stretched out by the bones of the arm and hand. The long bones of the fourth finger supported at least half of the wing's length. The first three fingers formed small claws about halfway along the front of the wing.

The skeleton of a pterosaur shows that it was probably a strong flier. Pterosaur bones were thin, fragile and full of holes to make them light. The skull was long and pointed. The shoulder bones and muscles were very strong. This meant that pterosaurs probably flapped their wings to fly. For a long time, however, scientists thought that pterosaurs could only glide through the air.

Eudimorphodon's skeleton

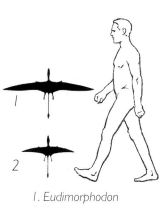

1. *Eudimorphodon*
2. *Peteinosaurus*

Peteinosaurus
This pterosaur had long fangs at the front of its mouth and smaller pointed teeth behind. This indicates that it may have been an insect-eater, feeding on large beetles and cockroaches.

WHERE DID THEY LIVE?

● *Eudimorphodon* and *Peteinosaurus*

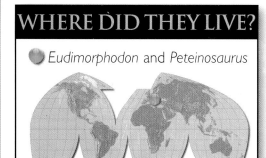

Earliest pterosaur

Eudimorphodon *was about the same size as a large seagull. It had sharp teeth that were used for grabbing wriggling prey. The teeth were unusual because they had more than one cusp (point). Most pterosaurs had simple, cone-shaped teeth. As Eudimorphodon got older, its teeth changed shape. Young ones may have fed on insects, such as dragonflies. Adults may have hunted fish.*

INTERNET LINKS

www.enchantedlearning.com/subjects/dinosaurs/dinos/Pterosaur.shtml
An introduction to pterosaurs, with a classification of the main forms.

www.bj.canon.co.jp/english/3D-papercraft/biology/index06.html
Make your own model of *Eudimorphodon* out of paper. Full instructions are provided with outlines to cut out.

FACTFILE: EUDIMORPHODON

Lived: 220 million years ago

Group: Ramphorhynchoidea

Size: 1 m wingspan

Weight: 600 g

Discovery: 1973, Cene, northern Italy

Diet: insects and fish

Special features: multi-pointed teeth

Name means: 'true two-form tooth'

HOW DO I SAY THAT?

EUDIMORPHODON
YOO-DIE-MORF-OH-DON

PETEINOSAURUS
PET-INE-OH-SAW-RUS

FOOD FOR FISH?

A fossil specimen of the Triassic pterosaur *Preondactylus* shows that it may have been caught by a huge predatory fish.

When *Preondactylus* was discovered in 1978, paleontologists were surprised to find all the bones squeezed into a tight ball. However, the skeleton was fairly complete, indicating that *Preondactylus* may have been swallowed by a predatory fish. The fish may have later spat out the undigestible bones. These would have sunk to bottom of the sea and fossilised in the bedrock.

Preondactylus was the third pterosaur to be found, after *Eudimorphodon* and *Peteinosaurus*. The discovery, while exciting and rare, did not further scientists' knowledge about the pterosaurs. It seems that the first pterosaurs were a group of reptiles with well-developed flight features, whose origins remain a bit of a mystery. The hunt for their ancestors in older rocks continues.

Caring parent
Preondactylus was a small pterosaur, about the same size as a pigeon. It had short wings and its jaws were lined with sharp, pointed teeth of different lengths. It is not clear whether Preondactylus *fed on insects or fish. Like birds today, mothers may have cared for their babies that are too young to fly.*

FACTFILE: PREONDACTYLUS

Lived: 220 million years ago

Group: Ramphorhynchoidea

Size: 45 cm wingspan

Weight: 300 g

Discovery: 1978, Preone, northern Italy

Diet: insects or fish

Special features: teeth of different lengths

Name means: 'Preone finger'

Unusual end

Did Preondactylus *meet an untimely end? Fossil evidence suggests that the pterosaur was eaten by the huge fish* Saurichthys, *which then spewed out the crushed bones.*

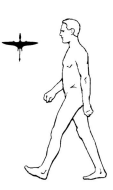

Preondactylus

WHERE DID THEY LIVE?

⬤ *Preondactylus*

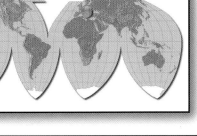

FISH-EATING PTEROSAURS

Pterosaurs spread all over the world during the Jurassic Period. The earliest Jurassic pterosaur was the long-tailed *Dimorphodon*, a relative of *Peteinosaurus*.

The first *Dimorphodon* fossils were discovered in 1828 on the south coast of England by the British fossil collector Mary Anning. She is famous for discovering fossils of icthyosaurs and plesiosaurs – giant reptiles that lived in the sea.

Dimorphodon had a relatively large head. The skull was not as heavy as it looked because it was full of hollow spaces. The sides of the head and beak may have been brightly coloured like puffins and toucans today. *Dimorphodon* had sharp, pointed teeth, which indicates that it was a fish-eater. It might have been hit by a large wave while hunting for food.

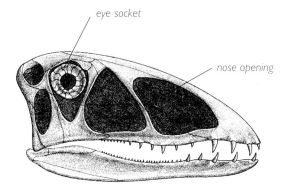

eye socket

nose opening

Big mouth
Dimorphodon *had two types of teeth used to grab and hold on to slippery fish.*

HOW DO I SAY THAT?

● DIMORPHODON
DIE-<u>MORF</u>-OH-DON

INTERNET LINKS

🔘 www.ucmp.berkeley.edu/diapsids/pterosauria.html
   A detailed review of Jurassic and Cretaceous pterosaurs.

🔘 www.wings.avkids.com/Book/Animals/intermediate/ancient-01.html
   All about how pterosaurs flew – basic aerodynamics.

Steering clear

Dimorphodon *had a long, stiff tail, which may have had a diamond-shaped vane at the end. The tail was probably used as a rudder to help the pterosaur steer as it flew in gusty winds.* Dimorphodon *had long fingers and claws on its hands. They were probably used to climb over rocks or trees.*

Dimorphodon

FACTFILE: DIMORPHODON

🔘 Lived: 200 million years ago

🔘 Group: Rhamphorhynchoidea

🔘 Size: 1 m wingspan

🔘 Weight: 1 kg

🔘 Discovery: 1828, Dorset, England

🔘 Diet: fish

🔘 Special features: deep jaws; spaced, sharp teeth

🔘 Name means: 'two-form teeth'

13

FOSSIL WONDERS

Pterodactylus **is probably the best-known pterosaur. Its name gave rise to the pterodactyloid group of pterosaurs.**

The pterodactyloids dominated the Jurassic skies and probably evolved from the rhamphorhynchoids of the Triassic Period. Many pterosaurs lived in coastal areas or around lakes. They often fell into the water when they died. Some of the best pterosaur fossils, such as those of *Pterodactylus* and *Rhamphorhynchus,* were discovered in the limestone deposits of Solnhofen in Germany. During the Jurassic Period, Solnhofen was covered by a lagoon. This created the perfect environment for fossilising the remains of pterosaurs.

The fossils of *Rhamphorhynchus* and *Pterodactylus* clearly show the skeleton and imprints of the wing membranes. Their discovery has contributed greatly to our knowledge of pterosaurs. Other fossils have been found on the south coast of England and in Tanzania, Africa.

FACTFILE: PTERODACTYLUS

Lived: 150 million years ago

Group: Pterodactyloidea

Size: 36 to 250 cm wingspan

Weight: 300 g to 2 kg

Discovery: 1784, Bavaria, Germany

Diet: fish

Special features: pointed snout, short tail

Name means: 'wing-finger'

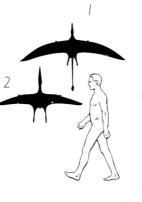

1. *Rhamphorhynchus*
2. *Pterodactylus*

Pterodactylus

Swooping over shallow waters, Pterodactylus probably snatched fish from the water and returned to land to feed. Fossils show that Pterodactylus had a throat pouch similar to that of a pelican, which may have been used to store food. Pterodactylus differed from rhamphorhynchoids such as Rhamphorhynchus. It had a short tail and longer head and neck. Its skull was lighter and met the neck at a right angle rather than a straight line. Pterodactylus also had longer wrist bones, so its fingers were farther down the wing compared to Rhamphorhynchus.

Rhamphorhynchus

Dozens of Rhamphorhynchus fossils have been found. These range from sparrow-sized baby skeletons to adults as big as an albatross.

Rhamphorhynchus had a long tail like the early pterosaurs. Its sharp teeth suggest that it was a fish-eater.

WHERE DID THEY LIVE?

● *Pterodactylus*   ○ *Rhamphorhynchus*

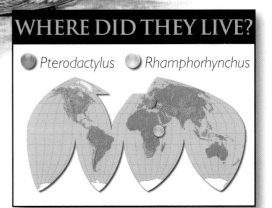

SHORT-LIVED PTEROSAURS

Above the Jurassic shorelines, the sky teemed with rhamphorhynchoid-type pterosaurs, many of whom died out by the end of this period.

Scaphognathus and *Anurognathus* have been found in only the rocks at Solnhofen in Germany. Along with other long-tailed pterosaurs, they both died out before the end of the Jurassic Period.

  Scaphognathus was similar to *Rhamphorhynchus*. It had long wings and a stiff tail with a steering vane at the end. However, *Scaphognathus* had a shorter head, a blunt mouth and few teeth. *Anurognathus* was a strange-looking creature that may have been the smallest pterosaur. Its wingspan of 50 centimetres made it the same size as a rook. Only one *Anurognathus* skeleton has been found – a single Late Jurassic fossil at Solnhofen.

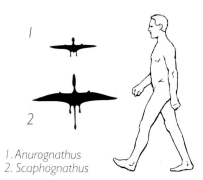

1. *Anurognathus*
2. *Scaphognathus*

Scaphognathus
This pterosaur had long, slender wings, so it could fly for long distances. Unlike fish-eating Rhamphorhynchus, *which had forward-sloping teeth, the teeth of* Scaphognathus *pointed upwards. It is not clear whether* Scaphognathus *fed on fish or insects.*

INTERNET LINKS

www.bbc.co.uk/dinosaurs/fact_files/scrub/anurognathus.shtml
Facts about *Anurognathus*, and a video clip of one of the heroes of the BBC's *Walking with Dinosaurs.*

www.ucmp.berkeley.edu/mesozoic/jurassic/solnhofen.html
Read all about the famous Solnhofen limestone quarries, where so many pterosaur fossils have been found.

Anurognathus

A small pterosaur with a blunt skull and short, peg-like teeth, which suggests it ate insects. It must have been an agile, graceful flier to hunt dragonflies and other flying prey. Its tail was unusually short, but other skeletal features make it a rhamphorhynchoid pterosaur rather than a pterodactyl.

Head

The fossilised skull of Scaphognathus shows that this pterosaur had slender, widely spaced teeth. The small holes around the outside edge of the upper jaw are the sockets for the 18 teeth.

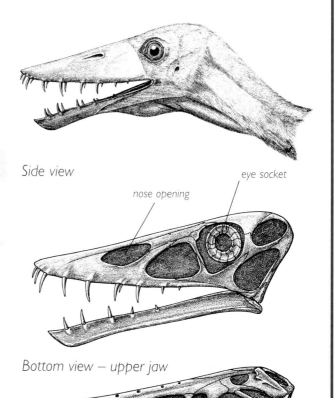

Side view

nose opening

eye socket

Bottom view – upper jaw

teeth sockets

HOW DO I SAY THAT?

ANUROGNATHUS
AN-YOO-ROG-NAY-THUS

SCAPHOGNATHUS
SKAF-OG-NAY-THUS

CREST-HEADS

Some pterodactyloid pterosaurs, such as *Germanodactylus* and *Gallodactylus,* had unusual crests on their heads.

When the fossils of *Gallodactylus* and *Germanodactylus* were discovered at Solnhofen in Germany, scientists thought they were *Pterodactylus* fossils. Both had the physical features of a typical pterodactyloid, such as a short tail. However, when paleontologists studied the skulls more closely, they discovered that these pterosaurs had strange horny crests on their heads.

1. *Gallodactylus*
2. *Germanodactylus*

Gallodactylus had a point at the back of its head that may have been used for signalling. *Germanodactylus* had a straight crest on the top of its nose. Scientists think that this may have been used as a 'cut-water'. This was a structure that stopped the head from wobbling as the pterosaur dived into the sea to snatch fish while hunting for food. Both pterosaurs died out by the end of the Jurassic Period.

Gallodactylus

A medium-sized pterosaur with a wingspan of 1.35 metres – much larger than a seagull. Gallodactylus had teeth at the front ends of its long, slender jaws. These pointed forward and would have been used to pluck slippery fish from the water.

WHERE DID THEY LIVE?

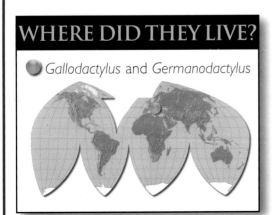

● *Gallodactylus* and *Germanodactylus*

HOW DO I SAY THAT?

● GALLODACTYLUS
GAL-OH-DAK-TIH-LUS

● GERMANODACTYLUS
JER-MAN-OH-DAK-TIH-LUS

- Lived: 150 million years ago
- Group: Pterodactyloidea
- Size: 1 m wingspan
- Weight: 1 kg
- Discovery: 1925, Bavaria, Germany
- Diet: fish
- Special features: pointed snout, crest on nose
- Name means: 'German finger'

Germanodactylus

This pterosaur lived on the shore but foraged out over the water for fish. Two Germanodactylus are shown here. One is using its strong finger claws to climb up the trunk of a tree. The other is hanging like a bat – by turning its feet backwards to get a good grip.

FISH-TRAPPERS

Ctenochasma **and** *Gnathosaurus* **were intriguing pterosaurs. They had a strange way of feeding – using their jaws to filter fish from the water.**

Only two or three fossils of *Ctenochasma* and *Gnathosaurus* were discovered in the limestone rocks of Solnhofen in Germany. Not only are they rare finds, they are also unusual pterodactyloids. They had extraordinary long heads with a broadened tip at the end of their beaks. The jaws were lined with hundreds of tiny, slender teeth that stuck out sideways like a comb. The teeth formed a trap when fishing for food. These pterosaurs fed by scooping up large mouthfuls of water. When they raised their heads, the water would drain out between their teeth. They then swallowed the sea creatures left behind in their mouths.

HOW DO I SAY THAT?

● **CTENOCHASMA**
STEN-OH-CAS-MAH

● **GNATHOSAURUS**
NATH-OH-SAW-RUS

Water filters
Ctenochasma *had over 250 teeth. It probably did not feed in flight but by swimming or wading in the shallow waters of the Solnhofen lagoon and other bodies of water.*

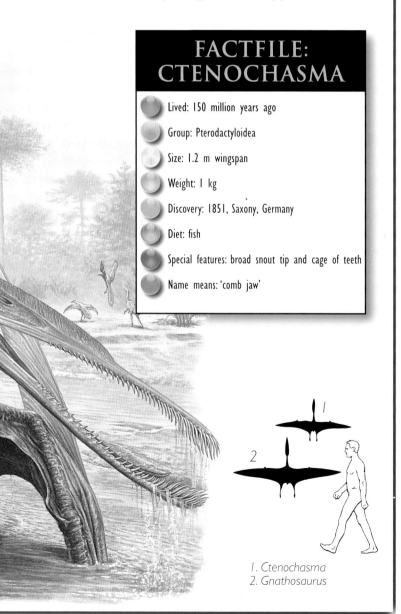

INTERNET LINKS

⦿ **www.dinosauria.com/dml/names/ptero.htm**
Find out about the origin of all the names
of pterosaurs and how to say them.

⦿ **www.kids.infonline.net/pteros.html**
Pictures of fossil pterosaurs and information
on how they were able to fly.

Gnathosaurus

*A large pterosaur, with a wingspan of 1.7 metres. When a piece
of its jaw was first discovered in 1832, it was mistaken for a
crocodile!* Gnathosaurus *had less teeth than* Ctenochasma *and
a more spoon-shaped jaw. It is shown below dipping its head for
fish. Another* Gnathosaurus *flies off in search of food elsewhere.*

FACTFILE: CTENOCHASMA

⦿ Lived: 150 million years ago

⦿ Group: Pterodactyloidea

⦿ Size: 1.2 m wingspan

⦿ Weight: 1 kg

⦿ Discovery: 1851, Saxony, Germany

⦿ Diet: fish

⦿ Special features: broad snout tip and cage of teeth

⦿ Name means: 'comb jaw'

1. Ctenochasma
2. Gnathosaurus

FURRY FLIERS

Fossil evidence shows that the pterosaurs *Sordes* and *Batrachognathus* were covered in hair.

Fossils normally show only the hard parts of an animal, such as the bones. The softer parts, such as the flesh and skin, usually rot away before they are preserved and become fossils. *Sordes* and *Batrachognathus* were found in rocks that were unusual because they were formed by the fine sediment deposits at the bottom of a lake. Paleontologists had found beautifully preserved fossils of plants and insects before discovering five or six pterosaur skeletons. When paleontologists studied the skeletons under a microscope, they could clearly see thick hair covering the back and neck, and thinner hair on the wings.

Sordes

Complete *fossil*
This is a drawing of a fossil of Sordes that was found in the Jurassic deposits of Kazakhstan in Asia. It shows the outline of the wings and thick hair covering the back.

HOW DO I SAY THAT?

● **BATRACHOGNATHUS**
BA-TRACH-OG-NATH-US
● **SORDES**
SOR-DAYS

1. *Sordes*
2. *Batrachognathus*

1

2

Sordes

This pterosaur was a small, long-tailed rhamphorhynchoid. It may have been a relative of another Jurassic pterosaur, Scaphognathus, discovered in Solnhofen deposits in Germany. Both have a similar head, upright teeth set far apart and relatively short wing fingers.

WHERE DID THEY LIVE?

Sordes and *Batrachognathus*

Batrachognathus

Incomplete fossils of another furry pterosaur – Batrachognathus – were found in the deposits in Kazakhstan. Its physical features suggest it was a close relative of Anurognathus. It had a short tail, broad head and frog-like mouth.

FACTFILE: SORDES

- Lived: 150 million years ago
- Group: Rhamphorhynchoidea
- Size: 60 cm wingspan
- Weight: 500 g
- Discovery: 1970, Kazakhstan, Asia
- Diet: insects
- Special features: broad wings, hair
- Name means: 'hairy devil'

WEIRD PTEROSAURS

Pterosaurs became even more diverse and amazing during the Cretaceous Period, which lasted from 150 to 65 million years ago.

The dsungaripterids were the first flying monsters. With wingspans of 3 metres, these pterosaurs were as big as today's largest birds – the condor or the albatross. Fossils of skeletons show that these pterosaurs had bizarre-shaped head crests and extraordinary snouts and jaws, which curved upwards. The shape of the jaws usually indicates how an animal lived and what it ate. *Dsungaripterus* had jaws lined with blunt bony knobs instead of teeth. The narrow pointed jaws may have been used to prise out shellfish from rocky crannies. Shells would have been crushed by the bony knobs in the mouth.

Fantastic head crests

Crests enabled pterosaurs to signal to each other and to identify members of their own species (kind). Some pterosaurs may have had crests to help them steer in the sky or through water.

WHERE DID THEY LIVE?

● *Dsungaripterus* and *Phobetor*

FACTFILE: DSUNGARIPTERUS

- Lived: 130 million years ago
- Group: Pterodactyloidea
- Size: 3 m wingspan
- Weight: 2 kg
- Discovery: 1964, Sinkiang, China
- Diet: shellfish or fish
- Special features: pointed, upturned snout
- Name means: 'Junggar wing'

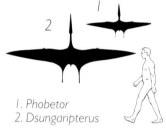

1. Phobetor
2. Dsungaripterus

Phobetor

Fossils of the pterosaur Phobetor *were found Mongolia.* Phobetor *was a relative of* Dsungaripterus, *which came from China.* Phobetor *was half the size of* Dsungaripterus *but had a similar head crest. Its jaws were straighter than those of* Dsungaripterus *and contained proper teeth instead of bony knobs.*

Dsungaripterus

HOW DO I SAY THAT?

- DSUNGARIPTERUS
  D-SUNG-AH-RIP-TER-US
- PHOBETOR
  FO-BET-OR

FILTER-FEEDERS

Pterodaustro fed like a blue whale does today – its huge jaws filtered fish from the sea.

Pterodaustro had an amazing set of bendy teeth in its lower jaw – more than 2000 of them. The teeth worked like a fishing net. The pterosaur dipped its jaw into the sea and skimmed along the surface of the water. Fish, shrimps and other sea creatures were trapped in the teeth and then swallowed. This is similar to the way blue whales feed today. Earlier pterosaurs, such as _Gnathosaurus_ and _Ctenochasma_ of the Jurassic Period, may have filtered their food in this way, too. However, they did not have quite as many teeth as _Pterodaustro_.

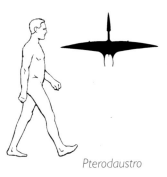

Pterodaustro

INTERNET LINKS

🌐 **www.carleton.ca/Museum/ptero/pterodaustro.htm**
Basic information about _Pterodaustro_, including a a great picture of this pterosaur.

🌐 **www.fernbank.edu/museum/pterosaurs.html**
Details of a museum exhibit showing a large flock of 21 _Pterodaustro_.

WHERE DID THEY LIVE?

🔴 *Pterodaustro*

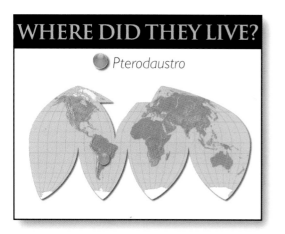

Weird teeth

These pictures of the head of Pterodaustro show its amazing teeth. When the jaws were shut, the lower teeth would stick out above the snout. The lower jaw had long, elastic bristles for teeth to filter sea creatures from the water. The upper jaw had small blunt teeth to chop up food.

Big differences

Pterodaustro *has been called the 'flamingo pterosaur' by scientists, because it had a very long head compared to the length of its body.*

FACTFILE: PTERODAUSTRO

- Lived: 140 million years ago
- Group: Pterodactyloidea
- Size: 1.3 m wingspan
- Weight: 3 kg
- Discovery: 1970, Argentina
- Diet: small fish and other sea creatures
- Special features: 2000 flexible, long teeth
- Name means: 'southern wing'

Feeding

Pterodaustro *squats and dips its lower jaw into the water to trap little sea creatures that float near the surface. This pterosaur may have skimmed for food by swinging its head from side to side to drain water out through its lower teeth.*

HOW DO I SAY THAT?

🔴 **PTERODAUSTRO**
TERO-<u>DAW</u>-STRO

FLYING GIANTS

The largest pterosaurs were *Pteranodon* and *Nyctosaurus*. They were almost as big as a bus!

When the first fossils of *Pteranodon* were found in North America in 1870, paleontologists were amazed at their size. All they had found was a bone from the hand, but they could see it was ten times the size of the same hand bone in a *Pterodactylus* skeleton. Paleontologists thought that the bone came from a pterosaur with a wingspan of at least 6 metres. More complete fossils of *Pteranodon* have now been found. These fossils indicate that the pterosaur had a bony crest at the back of its skull and no teeth in its mouth. *Nyctosaurus* was a smaller, toothless pterosaur from the same area as *Pteranodon*. It had a much shorter crest at the back of its head.

In late Cretaceous times, several species (kinds) of *Pteranodon* and *Nyctosaurus* lived over a shallow sea that covered the middle of what is now the USA. The largest species had a wingspan of 9 metres. This is much bigger than any living bird. With wings outstretched, it would have spanned the length of a bus!

HOW DO I SAY THAT?

● NYCTOSAURUS
NIK-TOE-SAW-RUS

● PTERANODON
TER-AN-OH-DON

1
2

1. *Nyctosaurus*
2. *Pteranodon*

WHERE DID THEY LIVE?

● *Nyctosaurus* and *Pteranodon*

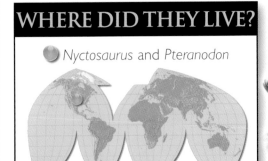

Heading the right way

Different species of Pteranodon had different shaped head crests. They could be long and pointed or tall and curved. The crests were hollow, so they were very light. It is not clear what they were used for. They may have helped to stabilise the head like a rudder during flight to keep it pointing into the wind.

Nyctosaurus

This slender-headed pterosaur was smaller than Pteranodon, with a wingspan of 3 metres. The name Nyctosaurus means 'naked reptile'.

FACTFILE: PTERANODON

- Lived: 100 to 70 million years ago
- Group: Pterodactyloidea
- Size: 6 to 9 m wingspan
- Weight: 10 to 16 kg
- Discovery: 1870, Kansas, USA
- Diet: fish
- Special features: huge wingspan, head crest
- Name means: 'toothless flier'

29

WINGED MONSTER

Pteranodon was thought to be the largest flying animal ever – until 1971, when an even larger pterosaur fossil was discovered.

Quetzalcoatlus was found on the 'big bend' of the Rio Grande river in the USA. The 'Texas pterosaur', as it was called, was a true flying monster. With a wingspan of 12 metres, it was twice as big as *Pteranodon.* It had a head crest and no teeth. Unlike *Pteranodon,* it had slender jaws that ended in a long, narrow pointed beak and an extremely long, rigid neck.

The discovery excited scientists. *Quetzalcoatlus* was not only the largest pterosaur to be found, it was also the last of the pterosaurs to live on Earth. It survived to the end of the Cretaceous Period, 65 million years ago, when all the pterosaurs and dinosaurs suddenly died out.

Quetzalcoatlus

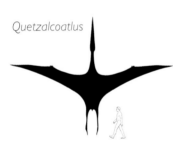

Quetzalcoatlus
This pterosaur had such huge wings that they would have broken if flapped too fast. Quetzalcoatlus probably glided on warm air currents, moving its wings slightly to adjust its position.

INTERNET LINKS

www.tyrrellmuseum.com/tour/quetzalcoatlus.html
Basic information and some amazing pictures of *Quetzalcoatlus.*

www.bbc.co.uk/dinosaurs/fact_files/volcanic/quetzalcoatlus.shtml
The BBC's *Walking with Dinosaurs* site, plus a short video clip of *Quetzalcoatlus.*

Fish- or flesh-eater?

Unlike most pterosaur fossils, Quetzalcoatlus was not found in sea bedrock but in river bed deposits. This means it could have been a meat-eating scavenger – feeding on dead animals. Alternatively, it may plucked fish from ponds.

FACTFILE: QUETZALCOATLUS

Lived: 75 to 65 million years ago

Group: Pterodactyloidea

Size: 12 m wingspan

Weight: 80 kg

Discovery: 1971, Texas, USA

Diet: possibly fish

Special features: huge wingspan, toothless jaws

Name means: 'Quetzalcoatl' was an Aztec god

INDEX